D1414783

PURSUING *THE* CHRIST

PRAYERS FOR CHRISTMASTIME

JENNIFER KENNEDY DEAN

NEW HOPE
PUBLISHERS
Birmingham, Alabama

New Hope® Publishers
P. O. Box 12065
Birmingham, AL 35202-2065
www.newhopedigital.com

New Hope Publishers is a division of WMU®.

The Library of Congress has cataloged the softcover edition as follows:

Dean, Jennifer Kennedy.
  Pursuing the Christ : 31 morning and evening prayers for Christmastime
/ Jennifer Kennedy Dean.
    p. cm.
  ISBN 978-1-59669-231-2 (sc)
  1. Christmas--Prayers and devotions. I. Title.
  BV45.D43 2008
  242'.33--dc22
                          2008023135

Cover design by the DesignWorks Group, www.thedesignworksgroup.com
Interior design by Sherry Hunt

Artwork on pages 13, 45, 75, and 101 by Kim Pierce; kimpiercedesigns@earthlink.net
Acrostic poems on pages 13, 45, 75, and 101 by Jennifer Kennedy Dean

ISBN-10: 1-59669-320-7
ISBN-13: 978-1-59669-320-3

N124127 • 1011 • 5M1

---------- TABLE OF CONTENTS ----------

Advent is the traditional term for the season of anticipation leading up to Christmas, the celebration of Christ's coming into the world. Observed as early as the fifth century, Advent today generally refers to the four weeks preceding December 25. The word *advent* has its root in the Latin word *adventus*, which means "coming." The biblical parallel is the Greek word *parousia*, used in the New Testament to refer to Christ's Second Coming. Advent, whether in reference to His first coming or Second Coming, is about Jesus breaking into our world.

Christmas is the day we have marked on our calendars to celebrate that pivotal event upon which all of human history hangs. On a certain day in time and space the eternal Word came into our view, clothed in flesh and born of a woman. In marking time, there is before, and there is after. All of time is measured from the moment when the Word became flesh and took up residence among us.

In our culture, we are easily distracted from the celebration's true purpose. Too many of us know that the Christmas season can quickly disintegrate into a time of stress, greed, busyness, competition, and emotional overload. To guard against the danger of overlaying the holy with the mundane, I offer you this little book. I invite you to begin each day of this Advent season not with to-do lists and shopping lists but with your heart anchored on the one Gift, who left His throne from which He heard the continual cry of "Holy, holy, holy" to take on a man's frame and hear instead,

"Crucify Him!" (Revelation 4:8; Matthew 27:22–23).

> *"Behold, the virgin shall be with child, and bear*
> *a Son, and they shall call His name Immanuel,"*
> *which is translated, "God with us."*
> —Matthew 1:23 (NKJV)

The moment of His Advent is introduced with the word *behold*. Quoting the prophet Isaiah, the angel used the Hebrew word for "behold"—*Hineh!* It is a word that alerts the hearer: "What I am about to announce is unbelievable, beyond comprehension, extraordinary." Listeners are tuned in, eagerly listening, taking in every word.

My son Brantley, a graduate student at Duke Divinity School, explains it this way:

> It is a word meant to provoke surprise and anticipate the extraordinary. We are accustomed to reading this word in translation as *behold*. Yet this word has little traction with modern English speakers and readers. When a young lover proposes marriage to his would-be bride and presents a dazzling diamond ring, *behold* would likely fail to capture the moment. When the Red Sox were liberated from generations of Yankee tyranny in dramatic, quintessential come-from-behind and bottom-of-the-ninth fashion, *"Behold! Behold!"* would have been fatal to the career of any color commentator. No, *behold* passes too easily through us, failing to register anything that would amount to true

beholding. Perhaps, by way of a colloquialism, our initiation into this text would be better served by imagining it begins with a rowdy: "Can you *believe this*?!" Here is the notion that we are introduced to something unfathomable—in fact, *un*believable.

It is nearly unbelievable—the wonder of the Advent of the Promised One, longed for through generations, now arriving in the context of human history. This Christmas season, be sure *not* to lose the wonder of the Wonderful by getting mired in the mundane.

THE FLESHED WORD

The Word became flesh and took up residence among us.
—John 1:14

The first newborn cries that echoed through a stable in Bethlehem were the announcement that human hearts had been longing to hear, even without being able to name the longing. God had come near. The Word had become flesh.

Jesus came to earth and took upon Himself the constraints of space and time. Born unceremoniously in a stable, His birth was greeted with stable smells and cattle lows. But that hidden moment, noticed by no one of consequence in the world's estimation, is the moment that defines all other moments. The Word became flesh and made His home among us.

A word is the expression and communication of a thought. Jesus embodied all the thoughts of God. He is every thought God has ever had, revealed in high-definition visual.

> *How precious to me are your thoughts, O God!*
> *How vast is the sum of them!*
> *Were I to count them,*
> *they would outnumber the grains of sand.*
> —Psalm 139:17–18 (NIV)

As you traverse this Christmas season, let these short, prayerful meditations open your heart to hear the thought that the Word is speaking to you. Read each day's beginning Scripture(s) in the morning and again in the evening. Press your ear to the Father's heart and draw close to Him as you read through this book. Let His thoughts become precious to you.

Celebrate this Christmas season with Christ in view.

Joy in the heavens and peace on Earth. For unto us a Son is given. Unto us a child is born. And He will Save His people from their sins.

Jennifer Kennedy Dean

All this took place to fulfill what the Lord had said through the prophet: "The virgin will be with child and will give birth to a son, and they will call him Immanuel"—which means, "God with us."
—Matthew 1:22–23 (NIV)

MORNING

Jesus, You are "God with us." I cannot quite grasp the fullness of it. Something more than God somewhere in the vicinity. More than God down the street. More than God within shouting distance. God *with* us.

On that night in a stable in Bethlehem, from earth's view, a baby was born. From heaven's view, You, God the Son, voluntarily left Your rightful place on the universe's throne, left the riches and the unimaginable glory that were Your own possessions, left the sound of praise and worship that surrounded You day and night— left it all to be with us.

What must that moment have been like? When heaven's great Treasure shed His kingly grandeur and donned mere clay, did the angels for a moment hold their breath and look on in astonishment? When He who was from the beginning took upon Himself the form of a servant, did the eternal realm halt—just for a heartbeat—and stand speechless with wonder? When the King of kings exchanged His majestic robes for swaddling clothes, surely it was the most beautiful, awe-inspiring moment in all eternity.

On earth, it was a little-noticed event. A young peasant couple and a few poor shepherds were the only witnesses to an ordinary birth in an ordinary place at an ordinary time. No pomp or ceremony. No grand announcement to a waiting crowd. No dancing in the streets.

In the heavens, that which looked ordinary from the earth was the spark for unparalleled celebration (Hebrews 1:6). It was something never before seen and never to be seen again—when the King became a servant.

> He so loved us that, for our sake,
> He was made man in time,
>   although through him all times were made.
> He was made man, who made man.
> He was created of a mother whom he created.
> He was carried by hands that he formed.
> He cried in the manger in wordless infancy,
>   he the Word,
> without whom all human eloquence is mute.
> —Augustine, Sermon 188, 2

---------- **THOUGHT FOR THE DAY** ----------

When the King of kings exchanged His majestic robes for swaddling clothes, surely it was the most beautiful, awe-inspiring moment in all eternity.

1

EVENING

> *"God with us."*
>
> *"In the beginning was the Word, and the Word was with God, and the Word was God. He was with God in the beginning"* (John 1:1–2). *You, the Son, were with Your Father from before the beginning. The One who was with God, came to be with us.*

Can our English word *with* capture it? Does it mean "with me" like someone next to me? No, nearer than that. Does it mean "with me" like someone holding me in tight embrace? No, nearer than that. "With me" like the blood in my veins? No, nearer still. "With me" like the beat of my heart? No, nearer, nearer.

"I no longer live, but Christ lives in me" (Galatians 2:20). *With* me becomes *in* me. When You, *God with us,* were born on that night long ago in a place far away, You opened the way for heaven to invade earth and earth to experience heaven. It was ultimately the birth of my salvation. The first step in that grand eternal plan that would make it possible for You, Jesus, to be closer than the breath in my body, to be Christ in me. You are no faraway deity waiting for me to find You. You are ***God with us.***

> God with us, Your desire for me compelled You to seek me out no matter the cost.
>
> God with us, You made Yourself knowable so that I could know You.
>
> God with us, You measured Your love for me against the splendor of heaven and chose me.

Little Baby, born in a stable, when You were still slick with Your mother's birthing fluids, pulling earth's air into Your new lungs for the first time, first hearing the sound Your vocal chords created in earth's atmosphere…even then, You were my salvation. Baby Jesus, may Your Spirit so align my life with Your willingness to embrace humility as a crowning achievement that this willingness becomes the evidence of Christ in me.

2

The historical record of Jesus Christ, the Son of David, the Son of Abraham.
—Matthew 1:1

MORNING

When You tell the story as it occurred on the earth side of the grand stage, You keep hinting at heaven's role. The record of the genealogy of Jesus Christ, born on earth to a mother named Mary and her husband named Joseph, though sparsely stated without elaboration, reminds me of what the Word made flesh has revealed to my heart. The details are there, but in shadow.

The genealogy reminds me that for generations—in fact since time began—You were in the process of fulfilling Your promise. While Your people thought You slow or even negligent, the promise was in progress. The ancestors through whom the Promised One would be revealed were being carefully hand selected. The ground-work was being laid. The picture was being framed and given texture and context. The story was being written, detail upon detail, building to its climactic event when the Word became flesh and made His dwelling among us.

I am reminded that You have the end firmly fixed from the beginning. You alone know everything that must be in place for the time to be ripe for the promise. You are always in the process of revealing the promise. You are careful and deliberate, but not slow.

Remind me, as I watch to see You move in my circumstances today, that I am not caught in any time-bound, earthbound problem. I am not enslaved to any need that presents itself in my experience. You are at work in a bigger, broader universe, beyond what I can see.

By the time the promise is revealed in my life, it has been worked out through people, each one changed as she becomes part of the genealogy of the promise. Each one handpicked and carefully placed along the way. Each one blessed as the promise sweeps him up into its orbit and moves him to march to its eternal rhythm.

As with the Ultimate Promise—Jesus, the Promise of all promises—when my promise is revealed in my circumstances, it is not for me alone. It is not just for my satisfaction or for my fulfillment, but rather it is the Word made flesh. It is the Word of promise that is now made evident and made visible in my circumstances.

The earth was just the setting in which the Word made flesh could become visible. My little circumstances are just the setting in which Your Word to me can become visible. Remind me when I forget. You are always in the process of keeping Your promise. In my life, a promise is always in progress. Thank You.

-------- **THOUGHT FOR THE DAY** --------
My little circumstances are just the setting
in which Your Word to me can become visible.

EVENING

In the genealogy of Jesus Christ, the Holy One, You are intentional in highlighting five women. In a list of men, through whom the bloodlines would be officially traced, You insist on mentioning these women. Though the language does not dwell on them or seem to call undue attention to them, their very mention is like writing their names in neon lights.

- *"Judah fathered Perez and Zerah by Tamar"* (Matthew 1:3).

- *"Salmon fathered Boaz by Rahab"* (Matthew 1:5).

- *"Boaz fathered Obed by Ruth"* (Matthew 1:5).

- *"David fathered Solomon by Uriah's wife"* (Matthew 1:6).

- *"Jacob fathered Joseph the husband of Mary, who gave birth to Jesus who is called the Messiah"* (Matthew 1:16).

Embedded in the Christmas story, eternally linked to its telling, five particular women are noted. Each has this in common with the others: She is not a likely character to be put out on display and touted as part of the ancestry of Messiah. She is not famous like Sarah or Rachel. Excluding Mary, these women are flawed, either in character or bloodline. Ruth was a Moabite, so her lineage should have excluded her. Tamar, Rahab, and Uriah's wife each had her own scandal. Mary was a young peasant girl of no particular distinction. Yet, here they are, singled out for the distinctive honor of being mentioned in the genealogy of the Messiah.

In the gene pool of the Word made flesh, grace is a dominant gene. John 1:16–17 reads, *"Indeed, we have all received grace after grace from His fullness, for although the law was given through Moses, grace and truth came through Jesus Christ."* Born again into Your bloodline, grace flows to me, through me, and from me.

Jesus Christ, Son of God, let the grace that I receive out of Your fullness spill out in torrents of grace to those around me. When I am tempted to hide or disguise the circumstances in my life when grace was most evident against the background of my sin, let me instead point to my failures to say, "Look what grace did!" Let me tout the history of Your grace in my life without shame.

"I am the Lord's slave," said Mary. "May it be done to me according to your word."—Luke 1:38

MORNING

Mary, betrothed to Joseph, no doubt got caught up in her preparations for the wedding ceremony and her day-dreams about being a wife. Learning from her mother and the women of the town the skills she would need to make a home and raise a family, her thoughts were occupied with her plans for her life. The way she imagined her life probably had small boundaries. She did not give even a thought to how she might impact all humankind from creation until the end of time. She more than likely just wanted a cozy home and a loving husband and some children to care for.

Into her ordinary plans for an ordinary life, Your messenger appeared. *"And the angel came to her and said, 'Rejoice, favored woman! The Lord is with you.' But she was deeply troubled by this statement, wondering what kind of greeting this could be"* (Luke 1:28–30). *"Favored woman,"* Gabriel called her. She was picked out, chosen, blessed.

Then the angel spoke further:

> *Do not be afraid, Mary, for you have found favor with God. Now listen: You will conceive and give birth to a son, and you will call His name JESUS. He will be great and will be called the Son of the Most High, and the Lord God will give Him the throne of His father David. He will reign over the house of Jacob forever, and His kingdom will have no end.* —Luke 1:30–33

Perhaps her mind raced trying to grasp what she was hearing and seeing. Her pulse quickened, her heart hammered, her face flushed. She was flustered and confused and, maybe, a little frightened. One question tumbled over another in her mind, but the one that found expression on her tongue was this: *"How can this be, since I have not been intimate with a man?"* (Luke 1:34).

But somehow the reality of Your call on her life settled on her. You broke through her uncertainties and made Yourself heard and known. In the course of a conversation, all her carefully laid plans were upended and scattered, and Mary became someone altogether different. The old Mary—she of little, tightly held plans—was buried and a new Mary was born.

You reveal Yourself to be One who can use a life only after it has passed through death. Your favor on Mary would call her to die to her reputation, to her pride, to her expectations, to her caution. But out of death arose a life that You could use to do more than Mary ever imagined.

Today, I receive as a gift from You those places where You are calling me to die to my own little plans so I can be born into Your grand plan. I am Your slave. May it be done to me as You have said. May Your Word be brought to fullness in my life, though it calls me first to walk through death.

--------- **THOUGHT FOR THE DAY** ---------
May Your Word be brought to fullness in my life,
though it calls me first to walk through death.

EVENING

In a nothing village called Nazareth in a nothing region called Galilee lived a nobody peasant girl named Mary, who was betrothed to a nobody carpenter named Joseph. To her, You sent the great and glorious and beautiful angel Gabriel. To her, You announced the news that all creation longed to hear. You called her to the task to which every young Jewish girl longed to be assigned—to bear the Messiah. A nobody from nowhere.

The story is all about You. You are the only part of the story that is worth noting. You are the only Hero, the only Actor, the only Author. Just You.

As You reveal Your thoughts toward us, we are astounded to discover that You do not seek out the loftiest or the loveliest, but rather You find the lowliest and the lackluster. You do not need a grand setting in which to do Your work because You are the Grand Setting. Nothing to brag about except You.

*God has chosen the world's foolish things
to shame the wise, and God has chosen the
world's weak things to shame the strong.
God has chosen the world's insignificant and
despised things—the things viewed as nothing—
so He might bring to nothing the things that are
viewed as something, so that no one can boast
in His presence. But from Him you are in Christ
Jesus, who for us became wisdom from God,
as well as righteousness, sanctification, and
redemption, in order that, as it is written:*

The one who boasts must boast in the Lord.
—1 Corinthians 1:27–31

Baby in a manger, born in a barn. Call His name Jesus, because He has saved His people from their sin. He has broken every yoke and set captives free. He has revealed the invisible God, bright glory filtered through His body of flesh so we would not have to hide our faces from the unapproachable light.

Little baby, wrapped in swaddling clothes and lying on a bed of hay, sheltered in a stable, birth unnoticed by earth's inhabitants. What a setting in which to find wisdom in person, righteousness embodied, redemption manifested.

May I value what You value. May I see beauty and magnificence where You see them. May I seek, not the glitter and the glamour that others might admire, but the hidden majesty of things despised and viewed as nothing. This Christmas season, may I find true humility. Bowing before You, my heart echoes Mary's proclamation: I am Your slave. May it be done to me according to Your word.

*"The Holy Spirit will come upon you, and
the power of the Most High will overshadow
you. Therefore the holy One to be born will be
called the Son of God....For nothing will be
impossible with God."*
—Luke 1:35, 37

MORNING

You never promise anything that You do not have all the
power necessary to accomplish. Mary could not help
but wonder how such a thing—a virgin bearing a son—
could be accomplished. The biological world did not
offer a way. The usual processes of procreation rendered
such a thing impossible.

Where the world has no way and no process, You
have a way. You are the way. By the exercise of Your
power and the experience of Your presence that which
was not so becomes so. Your voice calls into being that
which was not. You are the way.

Mary, familiar with the Hebrew Scriptures, heard
their echoes in Gabriel's words. *"The Holy Spirit will
come upon you."* In those words she heard the strains of
familiar thoughts: *"The Spirit of God was hovering over
the surface of the waters"* (Genesis 1:2).

And when she heard, *"And the power of the Most High
will overshadow you,"* did that phrasing turn her mind to
the cloud of glory so familiar to her forefathers: *"The glory
of the Lord settled on Mount Sinai, and the cloud covered
it for six days"* (Exodus 24:16). *"The Lord came down in
a cloud, stood with him there, and proclaimed His name
Yahweh"* (Exodus 34:5). In the words that Gabriel spoke,

Mary heard You say that Your power and Your presence are the necessary factors to bring Your promise into being. Nothing will be impossible for You.

You promise the impossible. You never speak a word that does not carry Your guarantee in it. You never speak a word that is not fully backed up by Your power.

You are the same God who spoke through Gabriel to Mary. When you speak to me, your words have the same guarantee. Whatever You promise, You perform. Why do I think I have to be able to see a way? You do not call me to believe based merely on evidence; You call me to believe things that are impossible. By the exercise of Your power and the experience of Your presence, nothing will be impossible.

--------- **THOUGHT FOR THE DAY** ---------
Whatever God has promised, He will perform.

EVENING

As I consider the wonder of Jesus, whose body was formed in the womb of Mary, I find myself longing for the character of the Christ to be formed in me.

Like Mary, I embrace Your promise: *"But you will receive power when the Holy Spirit has come upon you"* (Acts 1:8). Like Mary, I declare myself Your servant. Like Mary, I want Your Word to be accomplished in my life. *"Blessed is she who has believed that what the Lord has said to her will be accomplished!"* (Luke 1:45 NIV).

How fully did Mary have to yield to You? Did she find new ways every day to surrender? As a teenage girl on the cusp of adulthood, she surely did not see the whole picture on that one day. The surrender must have continued and deepened all her life. How often was she surprised at the things she had thought she could hold on to, but found she had to yield. She did not just believe You once in one bright shining moment, but she had to keep believing You anew.

I pray that You will keep me in the path of surrender *"until Christ is formed in [me]"* (Galatians 4:19). The most impossible thing I can imagine is that I could be fully yielded in every way—that my stubborn, prideful, resistant self could be reformed by the presence of Christ in me. But *"nothing is impossible with God"* (Luke 1:37 NIV).

Holy Spirit, come upon me, hover over me, over-shadow me. Fill me with Your power and Your presence. Impregnate me with the life of Christ. I believe that what You have spoken will be accomplished.

"She will give birth to a son, and you are to name Him Jesus, because He will save His people from their sins."
—Matthew 1:21

The mystery of godliness is great: He was manifested in the flesh.
—1 Timothy 3:16

The Father has sent the Son as Savior of the world.
—1 John 4:14

MORNING

On the night of Your birth, who could have imagined the events that had been set in motion? Could Mary, who had heard and seen Your angel and to whom the promise had been spoken—could even she have guessed what her last, long birth pang had instigated? She had the broad outline. She knew the general direction. But even Mary could not fathom the wonderful plan of outrageous grace by which her little baby would save His people from their sins.

When Your Incarnation began as a formless group of cells in Mary's womb, my salvation had already begun. Before Your little toddler feet ever took their first step, Your walk up Calvary's hill had commenced. When You moved from Mary's womb into the expanse of earth, You were taking the first step toward the Cross.

The purpose for Your birth was Your death. The purpose for Your death was Your resurrection. The purpose for Your resurrection was my salvation.

O holy night! Glory to God in the lowliest.
It was for me
He took on the time and space constraints of earth
Let a veil of flesh conceal His worth
Set redemption's plan in motion with His birth
It was for me

It was for me
He gave up His flesh, an offering for my sin
Let God's wrath toward me be spent on Him
Poured out His Life so my life could begin
It was for me

It was for me
He threw off the time and space constraints of earth
Shed His veil of flesh, revealed His worth
Opened up for me the way to Spirit-birth
It was for me

--------- **THOUGHT FOR THE DAY** ---------
The purpose for Your birth was Your death.
The purpose for Your death was Your resurrection.
The purpose for Your resurrection was my salvation.

5

EVENING

And the Father sent forth His firstborn Son
And wrapped Him in flesh

    And laid Him in a manger.
The Father sent His Son—
He took His infinite worth
And the brightness of His glory
And His majesty and power
And hid them behind a veil of humanity,
Frail and weak
    And laid Him in a manger.

The Father sent the Son—
His Everything; the Storehouse of His riches;
The Living Word; the Eternal Life;
The One for whom all the angels sang
And all the sons of God shouted for joy—
    And laid Him in a manger.

The Father took the Son—
His unblemished flesh,
His humanity, pure and holy—
    And laid Him on the altar.
And the nails that pierced the hands of the Son
Pierced the heart of the Father.

Father, let the outrageous love You demonstrated in the incarnation of Your Son blind me to any desire but my desire for You.

He was in the world, and the world was created through Him.
—John 1:10

In these last days, He has spoken to us by His Son,…through whom He made the universe.
—Hebrews 1:2

And one Lord, Jesus Christ, through whom are all things.
—1 Corinthians 8:6

All things were created through Him, and apart from Him not one thing was created that has been created.
—John 1:3

By Him everything was created, in heaven and on earth, the visible and the invisible, whether thrones or dominions or rulers or authorities—all things have been created through Him and for Him.
—Colossians 1:16

Morning

Every cell and molecule, every atom, every neutrino, every particle of earth is of Your own design. You thought it and then formed it. You meticulously set each piece into place, ordering the universe perfectly.

Your creation is so vast that only now have we begun to get a dim glimpse of its expanse—universes and planets and suns and moons and stars beyond the ones we inhabit, and others no doubt yet undiscovered. You, the Eternal Word, created everything *just by voicing*. That creative voicing thundered with such majesty and authority that universes sprang up farther than our eyes will ever be able to see.

Of all creation, You formed a single planet and designed it to be the cradle for Your Incarnation.

You chose one planet. You chose one nation on that planet and appointed it one patch of land as its country. You chose one woman from that nation. You chose one spot in that country. You chose all this for the great unveiling, the big reveal.

No one has ever seen God. The One and Only
Son—the One who is at the Father's side—
He has revealed Him.
—John 1:18

You, Creator and Ruler of all the universe, entered Your creation incognito. Who would have recognized the In-the-Beginning God in the form of a little baby lying in a feeding trough on a bed of hay in a lowly stable in a little village in a little country on a little planet?

There You were—revealing God, unveiling love and compassion, introducing Your creation to the heart of its Creator.

You left all fullness to come to my emptiness.
—Philippians 2:7

You left Your riches to enter my poverty.
—2 Corinthians 8:9

You left Your throne to become a servant.
—Matthew 20:28

You left the glory You had with the Father before the world began to participate in my unglorious humanity.
—John 17:4–5

When You created in the beginning, You were creating the platform, setting the scenery in place, and blocking the stage where the story of redemption would be enacted. Everything was made through You and *for* You.

I was created through You and for You. In all the universe and all the range of time and space, You strategically created me and assigned me a role in Your redemption story. Every cell of my body is Your creation and Yours to command. Help me reveal You. I am Your slave. May it be done to me according to Your Word.

--------- **THOUGHT FOR THE DAY** ---------
You strategically created me and assigned me a role in Your redemption story.

EVENING

In *The Jesus I Never Knew*, Philip Yancey describes how he came to better understand the Word-made-flesh concept:

> I learned about incarnation when I kept a salt-water aquarium. Management of a marine aquarium, I discovered, is no easy task. I had to run a portable chemical laboratory to monitor the nitrate levels and the ammonia content. I pumped in vitamins and antibiotics and sulfa drugs and enough enzymes to make a rock grow. I filtered the water through glass fibers and charcoal, and exposed it to ultraviolet light. You would think, in view of all the energy expended on their behalf, that my fish would at least be grateful. Not so. Every time my shadow loomed above the tank they dove for cover into the nearest shell. They showed me one "emotion" only: fear. Although I opened the lid and dropped in food on a regular schedule, three times a day, they responded to each visit as a sure sign of my designs to torture them. I could not convince them of my true concern.
>
> To my fish I was deity. I was too large for them, my actions too incomprehensible. My acts of mercy they saw as cruelty; my attempts at healing they viewed as destruction. To change their perceptions, I began to see, would require a form of incarnation. I would have to become a fish and "speak" to them in a language they could understand.

You came to us, whom You had created, so that we could know You and see You and touch You. You were willing to lay aside Your position in the heavens to position Yourself in a manger. No matter how many ways I say it, the reality of Your love astounds me.

> He by whom all things were made was made one of all things...He Who fills the world lays in a manger, great in the form of God but tiny in the form of a servant; this was in such a way that neither was His greatness diminished by His tininess, nor was His tininess overcome by His greatness.
> —Augustine, Sermon 187 1.1

Only You could have devised and then implemented such a plan. Only You could have found the way for heaven to invade earth, not through force or might, but through a tiny newborn baby.

Your entry points in my life are not the things about me that are strong. Those things have the potential to keep my life closed to Your appearing. Your entry points into my life are those places where I am weak. Fill my weaknesses with Your power.

I join my voice to the Apostle Paul's:

> *"I will most gladly boast all the more about my weaknesses, so that Christ's power may reside in me. So because of Christ, I am pleased in weaknesses, in insults, in catastrophes, in persecutions, and in pressures. For when I am weak, then I am strong."*
> —2 Corinthians 12:9–10

*The time came for her to give birth. Then she
gave birth to her firstborn Son, and she wrapped
Him snugly in cloth and laid Him in a feeding
trough—because there was no room for them at
the inn.*
—Luke 2:6–7

MORNING

Such an economy of language pronounces so
momentous an event. No grandiose words or well-
turned phrases could have spoken more elegantly. The
facts speak for themselves. The wonder is not stirred
by the reporting, but by the act of eternal love. Two
simple statements and the story is reported. But these
two sentences describe the moment toward which all
of history had been building since the first molecule of
matter was spoken into being.

Anticipated and longed for by heaven and earth, this
action was so stunning that words could only detract.
*"God is in heaven and you are on earth, so let your words
be few"* (Ecclesiastes 5:2). How quick I am to speak
and to string words into sentences and spin sentences
into paragraphs to fill any void in chatter. But I see how
spectacularly the arrangement of a few words—nouns
left mostly unmodified and verbs left naked—speak the
stark and wonderful truth. Silence speaks that for which
words are worthless.

No words can ever express the enormity of the Word
made flesh lying in a manger. *"He is before all things,
and by Him all things hold together"* (Colossians 1:17).
But on that holy night in Bethlehem, You cooed and

cried and nursed at Mary's breast. Jesus, Your hands, which would soon feel the tear of nails, curled around her finger. Your feet, which would soon be pierced for my transgressions, kicked the air in awkward infancy. Your head, which would soon be gouged by thorns, lay peacefully in Mary's arms. No words. No words.

-------- **THOUGHT FOR THE DAY** --------
Let silence speak.

EVENING

When the time came for Mary to give birth, You, Father, had placed her in the exact location on planet Earth where You wanted Your Son born. Why would a young newlywed, heavy with her first child, climb up on a donkey and travel an arduous path to a place where no accommodations would be available? Because You laid it out long ago:

> Bethlehem Ephrathah,
> you are small among the clans of Judah;
> One will come from you
> to be ruler over Israel for Me.
> His origin is from antiquity,
> from eternity.
> Therefore, He will abandon them until the time
> when she who is in labor has given birth;
> then the rest of His brothers will return
> to the people of Israel.
> He will stand and shepherd them
> in the strength of Yahweh,
> in the majestic name of Yahweh His God.
> They will live securely,
> for then His greatness will extend
> to the ends of the earth.
> —Micah 5:2–4

You used the pettiness and greed of Caesar Augustus, the Roman ruler whose vanity compelled him to register and number the people under his rule in order to assure him the full amount of taxes to his treasury.

His demand that every Hebrew resident travel to the town of his heritage and register according to lineage put Mary and Joseph in Bethlehem on exactly the night You had arranged. You use even the tyranny of tyrants to accomplish Your plan in Your way and at Your time. You brought Mary to Bethlehem to register her openly as a descendant of King David, the line from which the Messiah would come. To establish His genealogy on the legal record, You worked everything out according to Your design.

When the time came for her to give birth—*when the time came*, not before or after—she did.

As I ponder Christmas and listen to Your thoughts, made knowable by the Word made flesh, I hear You saying this to me, "When the time comes." As carefully as You orchestrated the appearance of the Redeemer on the earth, so carefully are You orchestrating Your activity in my life. In the Incarnation, You revealed who You are. You are a God who plans and arranges and is always in control of both time and timing.

Oh, let my words be few, so that I can hear You as You whisper to me simple words, "When the time comes."

Heaven's Treasure,
the Father's
Only Son
partook of our
humanity
to impart peace
on
Earth

Jennifer Kennedy Dean

*For a child will be born for us, a son will be
given to us.*
—Isaiah 9:6

MORNING

Nothing is more full of pure, undiluted hope than the birth of
a baby. A fresh slate. A new beginning. A life at its genesis,
not yet wounded by the harshness of reality. No mistakes to
regret, no offenses to forgive. Defined only by potential and
possibility.

How perfect, Lord, that Your Advent took the form
of a newborn baby.

My mind's eye sees You: tiny, squirming, wrinkled,
held protectively in the arms of Your mother. I look
upon You with wonder that You would come in such
vulnerability and helplessness so I could know the
thoughts of God. The Word, fleshed in a newborn, speaks
to me today of new beginnings and reborn hope.

Surrounded by things that wear out and disappoint,
I forget how "new" feels. I settle for patched up and propped
up, losing sight of new. Relationships, dreams, even faith, if
I am honest—surfaces scarred and chipped by failures and
failings—become so familiar in their shabbiness that I leave
them in their diminished condition, accepting reality.

But today, with my heart gazing on Jesus in the form
of a newborn baby, I remember new. I remember that
the moment in which heaven and earth intersected, the
most holy event in all eternity, found its platform in a
newborn baby. I remember that when You—Most High
God, Creator of heaven and earth—revealed Yourself in
flesh, You proclaimed the possibility that all things could

be new and could be continually renewed. Always new.
If anyone is in Christ, there is a new creation;
old things have passed away, and look, new
things have come.
—2 Corinthians 5:17

Old things are passed away, all things are made new.
I am forgetting what lies behind and looking forward to
what lies ahead. New, and then new again—that is Your
gift to me today. A fresh slate, a new beginning, outrageous hope defined only by potential and possibility.

When the sun comes through the pane
And you feel that momentary sense of hope,
of expectation,
You have heard my voice and you have heard my
voice.
In the midst of wrapping buying scurrying
worrying
When you've wondered how to deal with yearly
mundane,
You have felt me under in over and around,
You feel my presence, feel my presence.
Advent time of bringing forth into the world
Advent time of newness truth and unexpected
calm.
—Rachel Holley

--------- **THOUGHT FOR THE DAY** ---------
A fresh slate, a new beginning, outrageous hope
defined only by potential and possibility is my gift from You.

EVENING

"Born for us…given to us," today's opening Scripture says.

A carefully given gift is an indication of the value the giver places on the recipient. A delighted recipient might greet a valuable gift with a gasp and an exclamation, "For *me*?" The giver is rewarded for the time, thought, and money invested in the gift by the recipient's spontaneous delight.

As I think this evening on Your unspeakable Gift, I let my mind wander, considering the careful, detailed preparation You made. I contemplate the patient advance work You did. I remember how You miraculously put each piece in place in its perfect time, all leading up to the moment when You would wrap Your Gift in flesh and lay Him in a manger.

I cannot imagine any reason for such an extravagant gift except Your love for me. When Your Word took flesh's form, it came as the most delightful surprise. Your word was loud and clear: *love.* If I had guessed at what Your word would be, I might have guessed some other word. I might have guessed something more fitting, like "I am so disappointed" or "You will pay for that!" or "Here is what you deserve." I would never have guessed that Your word, the thought You wanted me to know, would just be *love.*

God's love was revealed among us in this way: God sent His One and Only Son into the world so that we might live through Him. Love consists in this: not that we loved God, but that

He loved us and sent His Son to be the propitia-
tion for our sins.
—1 John 4:9–10

Knowing that You have given *to me* Your finest treasure, I can rest assured that You will not withhold anything good from me. You shower me mo-ment by moment with tokens of Your love. I pray that my eyes stay open to see the good and perfect gifts that are always flowing from You to me.

Your Gift is rooted in who You are, not in who I am. Your Gift tells me that Your love for me surpasses anything I could ever feel as love. The love that I am able to feel for You is only an echo of the love You have for me.

The indescribable gift You have given me consumes me, drawing from me all the love I am capable of returning. It leaves me breathless. Having fixed my eyes on Jesus, the Gift, I have but one response—for *me*?

*In the days of King Herod of Judea, there was
a priest of Abijah's division named Zechariah.
His wife was from the daughters of Aaron, and
her name was Elizabeth. Both were righteous
in God's sight, living without blame according
to all the commandments and requirements
of the Lord. But they had no children because
Elizabeth could not conceive, and both of them
were well along in years.*

*When his division was on duty and he was
serving as priest before God, it happened that
he was chosen by lot, according to the custom
of the priesthood, to enter the sanctuary of the
Lord and burn incense. At the hour of incense
the whole assembly of the people was praying
outside. An angel of the Lord appeared to him,
standing to the right of the altar of incense.
When Zechariah saw him, he was startled and
overcome with fear. But the angel said to him:*

*Do not be afraid, Zechariah,
because your prayer has been heard.
Your wife Elizabeth will bear you a son,
and you will name him John.*
—Luke 1:5–13

MORNING

Timing is everything. You arranged the Incarnation so
precisely that each piece of the puzzle had to fall into
place exactly at the appointed time. You do not depend

on chance or fortunes. You are never *hoping* for the best. You are *arranging* the best.

As for Zechariah and Elizabeth, You had them in mind from the beginning. Zechariah's division was on duty at just the right time. Was that by chance? When they cast lots to see who would enter into the sanctuary to burn incense—an honor that a priest hoped to have once in his lifetime—the lot fell in Zechariah's lap. Did it happen by chance?

"The lot is cast into the lap, but its every decision is from the LORD" (Proverbs 16:33). The reality of Your Word was fleshed out in real time when Zechariah was chosen by the casting of lots to be exactly where You wanted him when You wanted him there.

When You revealed Yourself in the form of beloved Jesus, every act of the story as it unfolded revealed that You are a God in control of the details. I embrace the reality of Your Word in my life today. In my life, You are the God in control, even of minutiae and happenings as random as a lot cast into the lap.

--------- **THOUGHT FOR THE DAY** ---------
God is in control, even of minutiae and
happenings as random as a lot cast into the lap.

EVENING

How long had Zechariah and Elizabeth prayed for a son? And when did they quit praying for a son?

Elizabeth was too old to conceive. The time had passed when Elizabeth could realistically hope for a son. She had lived since her days as a young bride with an unfulfilled longing—a longing she at some point had probably accepted as hopeless because her womb, as Sarah's womb had been so long ago, was "dead" (Romans 4:19). With Elizabeth's dead womb, hope died.

You started the Incarnation with a resurrection. John was the life that came from Elizabeth's dead womb. Life came out of death; such is resurrection. The Incarnation event was framed in resurrections.

What could be more final, and therefore more hopeless, than death? Yet when Your Word was revealed in the earth, You proclaimed Yourself as a God for whom death is not a dead end. Death of a womb, death of a dream, death of a hope, or death of a body—in Your hands, any death is a prelude to resurrection.

The tomb.
   Place of death
   Full of dark night
   And suffocating hopelessness.
   The end.

Became the Beginning
And the womb from which
Eternal Life emerged.

Thank You, precious Jesus, for resurrected hope.

"How can I know this?" Zechariah asked the angel. "For I am an old man, and my wife is well along in years."

The angel answered him, "I am Gabriel, who stands in the presence of God, and I was sent to speak to you and tell you this good news. Now listen! You will become silent and unable to speak until the day these things take place, because you did not believe my words, which will be fulfilled in their proper time."

Meanwhile, the people were waiting for Zechariah, amazed that he stayed so long in the sanctuary. When he did come out, he could not speak to them. Then they realized that he had seen a vision in the sanctuary. He kept making signs to them and remained speechless. When the days of his ministry were completed, he went back home. —Luke 1:18–23

MORNING

While Elizabeth was pregnant with a son, Zechariah was pregnant with silence.

You took away Zechariah's voice. You left him with no choice but to be still in Your presence. He could not influence events. He could not adequately express his opinions and preferences and ideas. You silenced him for nine months, the time of a pregnancy.

You never punish your children in anger. You discipline in love. Any discipline You impose is for the purpose of redemption.

*God disciplines us for our good, that we may
share in his holiness. No disci-pline seems
pleasant at the time, but painful. Later on,
however, it produces a harvest of righteousness
and peace for those who have been trained by it.*
—Hebrews 12:10–11 (NIV)

To what did Zechariah's silence give birth? His silence gave birth to obedience and to praise. Though his friends and neighbors thought the miraculous son should be named after his father, Zechariah obeyed Your angel Gabriel's command and named the baby John. *"Immediately his mouth was opened and his tongue set free, and he began to speak, praising God"* (Luke 1:64).

When I find myself in circumstances in which I seem to have no voice, no influence, no impact, teach me to surrender to the silence. Show me the way You redeem my circumstances and birth obedience and praise in me, sometimes by taking me out of the driver's seat and setting me aside in silence.

--------- **THOUGHT FOR THE DAY** ---------
When I find myself in circumstances
in which I seem to have no voice,
no influence, no impact,
teach me to surrender to the silence.

EVENING

I understand Zechariah. He heard Your Word, but what he *saw* seemed to render Your Word impossible. You promised that he would have a son, but he saw that he was an old man and his wife was well along in years.

What I see is not what I get.

When You work out Your Word in the earth's arena, what starts out as invisible takes on flesh. When Your promise connects with faith, the ingredients for a miracle are in place. If faith is a little slow in embracing, You are patient and determined. But Your way never changes. You promise a reality that is hidden from our sight and call out faith to grasp hold of Your Word. Then, when the time is right, that invisible promise becomes visible reality.

You make promises that seem to be contradicted by my circumstances. Just as You did with Zechariah, You pull faith from me patiently. When Your promise and my faith combine, miracles result.

You who found faith on the earth and connected it to Your promise, find faith in me. Even when my faith is tiny and weak and hidden, You see the little speck that just needs Your promises to bring it out of hiding. I embrace Your promises, though they may seem as impossible as a baby born to an aged, barren couple, because You are the God who *"calls things into existence that do not exist"* (Romans 4:17).

Because of our God's merciful compassion,
the Dawn from on high will visit us
to shine on those who live in darkness
and the shadow of death,
to guide our feet into the way of peace.
—Luke 1:78–79

The people walking in darkness
have seen a great light;
on those living in the land of darkness,
a light has dawned.
—Isaiah 9:2

Morning

Utter darkness is a prison. Unable to see the landscape, the person walking in darkness is held captive.

A person in darkness cannot venture forward because she cannot see the dangers in the way. The person cannot head toward a goal, because the possibilities that lie ahead are not visible. Darkness isolates, separating one person from another. Darkness hides reality and leaves a person enslaved to his own imaginations and perceptions of reality.

Darkness breeds fear and mistrust. As it turns out, the unenlightened imagination goes naturally to the worst possibilities and the most frightening scenarios.

We were born for light. You made us to crave the light. Light brings life to the cells and activates the processes of growth. Light is essential.

Until I saw You, I had never seen light. Until my heart found that light it craved, I was living in darkness and in the shadow of death. Bring Your light into every corner of my life. May I be fully set free from the prison of my darkness. Let Your light shine.

———— THOUGHT FOR THE DAY ————
Bring Your light into every corner of my life.

EVENING

You who in the beginning said, *"Let there be light"* (Genesis 1:3), came to earth to be Light: *"The true light, who gives light to everyone, was coming into the world"* (John 1:9).

In the manger, Light that had been eternally existent—of which the sun is but a pale shadow—lay sleeping. You are the true Light, whose being is glorious beyond our imaginations—so full of glory that You light the heavens just by existing. You were willing to veil that unapproachable light in a body of flesh to bring Light to earth.

When the Holy Spirit overshadowed Mary, were the words that created life in her womb the same words spoken in the beginning? *"Let there be Light."* And there *was* Light.

When light is present, darkness is not. Light and darkness do not coexist. Light dispels darkness simply by its presence. You separated light from darkness when You set the world in place (Genesis 1:4). *"Even in darkness light dawns for the upright, for the gracious and compassionate and righteous man"* (Psalm 112:4 NIV).

I celebrate You in my life, shining brightly on me, in me, through me. When I consider You snuggled in Your mother's embrace, I remember that You were willing to come into my darkness so I could know Light. Thank you, Jesus, that no matter what circumstances threaten to darken my life, I have hope because the Dawn from on high has made His way to me.

[H]e does not disdain to inhabit what he deigned to fashion; he does not think that it is undignified for him to touch flesh since he handled it in the past with his heavenly hand when it was in the form of dust.

He has come to your face, O man, because you were unable to reach his face, and he who was invisible has become visible for your redemption. The One besought by your ancestors has come. Listen to the voice of one who cries out, "Show your face, and we shall be saved."

—adapted from the works of Peter Chrysologus (406–450), from *A Classic Nativity Devotional* compiled by James Stuart Bell

After Jesus was born in Bethlehem of Judea in the days of King Herod, wise men from the east arrived unexpectedly in Jerusalem, saying, "Where is He who has been born King of the Jews? For we saw His star in the east and have come to worship Him." …

And there it was—the star they had seen in the east! It led them until it came and stopped above the place where the child was. When they saw the star, they were overjoyed beyond measure. Entering the house, they saw the child with Mary His mother, and falling to their knees, they worshiped Him. Then they opened their treasures and presented Him with gifts: gold, frankincense, and myrrh.

—Matthew 2:1–2, 9–11

MORNING

The wise men, astronomers who watched and studied the sky, headed east following a star. How many years had they watched and waited, longing to see that one star? Longing to receive the word of Your Advent? How long had they hoped for the Dawn from on high to break upon their darkness?

When they arrived at the humble home in which You lived, and saw You with Your simple peasant mother, Your surroundings were not even an issue to them. Your presence over-whelmed them. They were overjoyed beyond measure and fell to their knees and worshipped You.

They saw no castle for You as King, no robe or scepter or earthly throne, no attending servants, no army to command—no indications that You were King. Yet when they experienced Your presence and saw Your face, no one had to explain the protocol for them. There was but one response: worship.

Who has believed what we have heard?
And who has the arm of the LORD been revealed to?
He grew up before Him like a young plant
and like a root out of dry ground.
He had no form or splendor that we should look at Him,
no appearance that we should desire Him.
—Isaiah 53:1–2

Nothing was around You that would cause us to desire You. You were the only draw. All the riches and splendor of heaven were not around You, but in You.

Dear Savior, I want to be like the wise men. I do not want to be caught up in the trappings or distracted by the surroundings. Keep me focused fully on Your dear face. Let Your presence be what enthralls me. Everything else is just the wrapping, disposable and worthless when compared to the surpassing worth of knowing You. You are the One for whom my heart was made, and Your presence is all I need. You have birthed hope in me that lights every dark space and causes fear to flee.

THOUGHT FOR THE DAY

You are the One for whom my heart was made,
and Your presence is all I need.

EVENING

Seeing the star did not satisfy the longing in the wise
men. Observing it and studying it and contemplating it
did not suffice. Seeing the star awakened a hope that
drove the wise men to follow it wherever it led, because
it would certainly lead to You. It was not the star they
had been watching for all these years. It was You.

The star drew them. It hinted to them about
something beyond their observation. It called them to a
journey, the end of which would be Your very presence.
And nothing could stop them. The call and the pull was
stronger than any discouragement or uncertainty. You
are like a magnet to the hearts that hope in You. Just a
glimpse, and no earthly substitute will do.

> My hungry heart cries out for You.
> No earthly substitute will do.
> My life the bush, Your Life the Flame
> That leaves me nevermore the same.

Jesus, every glimpse I see of You causes me to want
more of You. This Christmas, season of wanting and
getting, show me Your star. Show me the path that has
You as its only destination.

> When therefore the first spark of a desire after
> God arises in your soul, cherish it with all your
> care, give all your heart into it, it is nothing
> less than a touch of the divine loadstone, that
> is to draw you out of the vanity of time into the
> riches of eternity. Get up therefore and follow it

as gladly, as the wise men of the East followed the star from heaven that appeared to them. It will do for you, as the star did for them. It will lead you to the birth of Jesus, not in a stable at Bethlehem in Judea, but to the birth of Jesus in the dark center of your own fallen soul.

—adapted from *The Spirit of Prayer* by William Law (1686–1761), from *A Classic Nativity Devotional* compiled by James Stuart Bell

The birth of Jesus Christ came about this way: After His mother Mary had been engaged to Joseph, it was discovered before they came together that she was pregnant by the Holy Spirit. So her husband Joseph, being a righteous man, and not wanting to disgrace her publicly, decided to divorce her secretly.

But after he had considered these things, an angel of the Lord suddenly appeared to him in a dream, saying, "Joseph, son of David, don't be afraid to take Mary as your wife, because what has been conceived in her is by the Holy Spirit. She will give birth to a son, and you are to name Him Jesus, because He will save His people from their sins."…

When Joseph got up from sleeping, he did as the Lord's angel had commanded him. He married her but did not know her intimately until she gave birth to a son. And he named Him Jesus.

—Matthew 1:18–21, 24–25

MORNING

Hopes were dashed. Joseph thought he was marrying a pious girl who was pure and virginal. Lord, I can imagine his confusion and hurt and, surely, anger when he first heard the news of her pregnancy. He had never anticipated such a betrayal and such a humiliation. As I ponder the way You worked out the unveiling of Your Word made flesh, I wonder why Joseph's experience unfolded as it did. Why did You not tell Joseph when You told Mary?

Why did You let him go through the death of his hopes?

And yet, I already sense the answer. You only allow death so You can bring resurrection. When Joseph's dashed dreams were replaced with Your dream for him, the hurt and confusion were left behind. He could only see the tiniest piece of the story, but You could give him the bigger picture, and that changed everything.

I imagine Mary in that time frame during which Joseph planned to divorce her secretly. Had she assumed, since she was highly favored and blessed among women, that she would not experience such hurt when she told Joseph her news? Did she have a crisis of faith during those hours of uncertainty? Did she wonder where You were at that time? Did she have to die a little more to her expectations of what it should be like to be the mother of Messiah?

More death gives way to more resurrection: less of Mary, more of You; less of Joseph, more of You.

Jesus, as You are being formed in me, I surrender to the disappointments along the way. I admit there are times when I think You must have forgotten me and left me to fend for myself, but deep inside I always know You are there. When disappointments loom large, remind me that I can only see the tiniest piece of the story. Remind me that if I could see what You see, it would all look different to me.

Less of me, more of You—this is my prayer.

-------- THOUGHT FOR THE DAY --------
When disappointments loom large,
remember that you can only see
the tiniest piece of the story.

EVENING

"Do not be afraid."

To Zechariah, You said, *"Do not be afraid."* To Mary, You said, *"Do not be afraid."* To Joseph, You said, *"Don't be afraid."* To the shepherds, You said, *"Don't be afraid."* (See Luke 1:13,30; Matthew 1:20; Luke 2:10.)

At every appearance, the first words delivered by Your messenger were, *"Do not be afraid."*

Afraid of what? I wonder. I am sure that the sight of a heavenly being in earth's sphere had to be so surprising and unexpected and so stunningly beautiful that it startled. But I am not sure that was the reason for those opening words.

You never appear in our lives just to startle us or entertain us or impress us. You come to call us to tasks so big we could never accomplish them and would never dare to undertake them on our own. You come to assign us a place in Your plan. And with Your command comes Your power.

You preface Your call on my life with the same statement: *"Do not be afraid."* You are not sending me out on my own to muddle through the best I can. You are inviting me to be the vessel through which You will work. You are inviting me to let You impregnate me with Your desires, gestate Your vision in me, and then bring it into the world through my life. A big call, but Your words introduce it: *"Do not be afraid."*

Jesus, in this Christmas season, let me embrace Your call without fear. *"'Not by strength or by might, but by My Spirit,' says the L*ORD* of Hosts"* (Zechariah 4:6).

Praise the Lord, the God of Israel,
because He has visited
and provided redemption for His people.
He has raised up a horn of salvation for us
in the house of His servant David,
just as He spoke by the mouth
of His holy prophets in ancient times;
salvation from our enemies
and from the clutches of those who hate us.
—Luke 1:68–71

Morning

Hope deferred, now fulfilled. You, the Redeemer God have proven Your Word true and have proven Yourself true to Your Word. You have raised up a horn of salvation for Your people.

The horn of an animal is its strength and its defense. The altar in the Temple had four horns, one at each corner—a foreshadowing and foretelling of this very event: Jesus, little baby in the manger, a horn of salvation raised up for His people.

When an animal gores its enemy, its horns are covered with the blood of that opponent. The blood on the horns of the triumphant animal proclaims its victory. But You Lord, the Horn of our salvation, are covered with Your own blood. Your own blood poured out for Your people turns back their enemy and lays low the adversary.

Baby Jesus, I imagine Your sweet baby face: contorted when You cry, delightfully toothless when You coo, alert and curious as You experience Your new surroundings.

In my imagination, I can feel Your soft baby skin and hear Your funny baby noises. I see Mary watching every change of expression with the wonder of a first-time mother. I watch the scene in my mind's eye, and I can hardly imagine that You are the Horn of salvation.

But I look longer and I see a shadow falls across the lovely Christmas scene. The shadow is cruciform and off in the distance; I can see the Cross, already present in Your birth, already making its claim on You, calling You. The blood running through Your darling newborn body will one day be spilt for me, for us. With Your own blood, You will redeem me and save me from my enemies and from the clutches of those who hate me.

O, Horn of my salvation, I worship You in this glad season, because in the shadow of the Cross that falls across the manger, I see my one and only hope.

--------- **THOUGHT FOR THE DAY** ---------
In the shadow of the Cross that falls across the manger,
see your one and only hope.

EVENING

"Just as He spoke by the mouth of His holy prophets,"
Zechariah declared as he prophesied (Luke 1:70).
It would happen just as You said.

You never leave us out of Your story. You always start
by making the promise, and so awakening expectation.
You pull us into the action, first by requiring faith in
something not yet seen, something impossible. Then
You encourage and uphold us as we walk that part of the
journey during which what You have promised seems
not to come and time passes and faith almost faints.
Then, in the fullness of time, that which You spoke, You
perform.

> *"I, the LORD, will speak whatever message I will*
> *speak, and it will be done."*
> —Ezekiel 12:25

> *"I watch over My word to accomplish it."*
> —Jeremiah 1:12

Jesus entered earth's atmosphere quietly one night in
Bethlehem's stable, and the promise You had first spoken
in the Garden of Eden (Genesis 3:15) was fulfilled.
A promise You had renewed through every generation.
A hope and expectation that You kept alive in Your
people. All the time, You were preparing the way for
the promise, laying the groundwork for its fulfillment,
readying the hearts of Your people.

Jesus, You are the proof that our God is a God whose promises are sure. When it looks to me as if You are neglecting Your promises, let my heart see You, the Promise, lying incongruously on a bed of hay, transforming the ordinary into the holy. My soul waits for the fullness of time.

PEACE

Participating in our
humanity, the
Son of God

Emptied Himself

and taking upon Himself
the form of
a servant

came from Heaven
to earth
to bring

Eternal Life

Jennifer Kennedy Dean

When the parents brought in the child Jesus to perform for Him what was customary under the law, Simeon took Him up in his arms, praised God, and said:
Now, Master,
You can dismiss Your slave in peace,
according to Your word.
For my eyes have seen Your salvation.
You have prepared it
in the presence of all peoples—
a light for revelation to the Gentiles
and glory to Your people Israel.
—Luke 2:27–32

MORNING

By the time Your promises are fulfilled, You have first created the expectation and fanned the flames of hope in those whose hearts are attuned to You. You have opened the eyes of faith in the one who looks to You. Take Simeon, for example—old Simeon, well along in years, righteous and devout. You had made him a promise that he would not die until his eyes had seen Your salvation.

On that day when Mary and Joseph brought their little baby to the temple courts, they were there to offer the customary sacrifices at the customary time in the customary way—an ordinary scene. Nothing outstanding or unusual was happening; nothing occurred to call Simeon's attention to the family from Nazareth.

Simeon was not alone at the temple. Others were there—many others, probably. They looked at the family from Nazareth, too, did they not? Yet only Simeon looked at the family and saw Your salvation. Only Simeon recognized in the flesh what his heart had been seeing in the Spirit for years.

At Simeon's age, it is likely that his eyesight had faded. He probably could not see as clearly as many of those at the temple that day. Yet, when he looked at what everyone else was looking at, he saw Your salvation. There You were, cloaked in the ordinary. Those focused on rites and ceremonies, those evaluating position and prestige—they missed You. Though You were right in their midst, they were blind to Your presence. But Simeon, whose spiritual sight was sharp, saw You clearly.

Simeon, when he saw You, proclaimed himself at peace. The sight of You, even in Your infancy, brought peace to Simeon's old heart.

Lord Jesus, in this Christmas season where we sing songs about peace but fill our days with chaos, let me see You in the ordinary. Let me recognize You in the comings and goings. Let me look beyond the glitter of the holiday and see the glory of Your presence. And I, too, will be at peace.

-------- **THOUGHT FOR THE DAY** ---------
Let me look beyond the glitter of the holiday
and see the glory of Your presence.

EVENING

Simeon took You up in his arms. What a moment that must have been for dear Simeon. With You balanced in the crook of his arm, pressed against his aged breast, Simeon looked into the face of his Savior.

How overcome he must have been. Surely tears flooded his eyes and tumbled down his craggy cheeks. He had to have felt that divine and eternal moment with his whole being. Simeon held his Salvation in his embrace and felt the Master's touch.

Peace, confidence, certainty; a sense of being settled and stable and safe; clarity about who is in charge; awareness of Your power—all of this is part of the peace I feel when I experience Your touch.

This Christmas season, when I fall into the well-worn patterns of my flesh—trying to measure up, trying to make everybody happy, trying to attend perfectly to every detail, trying to fulfill other people's expectations—capture my heart with Your touch. Bring peace to my thoughts with Your presence. "When my anxious thoughts multiply within me, Your consolations delight my soul" (Psalm 94:19 NASB). No matter what frenetic activity and insistent demands swirl around me, I want to be able to say, "My eyes have seen Your Salvation" (Luke 2:30). Let me be transfixed by Your face.

For the mind-set of the flesh is death, but the mind-set of the Spirit is life and peace.
—Romans 8:6

MORNING

Incarnate Word, You came to set my captive thoughts free and to captivate my restless mind and anchor it in You.

Without You, my thoughts were entangled by the dictates of my flesh. They poisoned and polluted my life. My thoughts were infused with the stench of death, corrupted, decaying, marching steadily toward the grave. The power of death spread to cover every pursuit, every relationship, every dream.

Then You came. Softly. Barely a ripple in the course of mankind's doings, yet a rip that reverberated through the heavenly realms and changed the balance of power for all eternity. With a battle cry that sounded to earthly ears like a newborn baby's whimper, You set in motion my redemption. The sound heard in the heavens that first Christmas moment was a victory shout that rattled the enemy's forces and insured their defeat.

I was death's child, sin's slave. No future but the grave. A mind managed by my flesh. Until You.

Jesus, thank You for recasting my thoughts into the mold of Yours. *"But we have the mind of Christ"* (1 Corinthians 2:16). Teach me how to receive that gift in its fullness. Make me so moldable that You can transform my heart completely until its thoughts and intents are reflective of Your life in me, Your peace in me.

######### **THOUGHT FOR THE DAY** #########
Make me so moldable
that You can transform my heart completely
until its thoughts and intents
are reflective of Your life in me,
Your peace in me.

EVENING

Having a mind that is set on the things of the Spirit brings life and peace. A set mind is established, fixed, focused, immovable, determined.

Your mind is set on me. Your heart has been fixed on me since before the world began. Your thoughts never wander from me. From before time began, You set Your mind toward the Cross and, with never-wavering love, took on earth's trappings to save me from death and its force in my life.

A Redeemer grew in Mary's womb; a body was knit together that would house the Prince of Peace. All the power heaven holds was contained in a body built of earth's stuff—all for the determined purpose of overcoming the death that held me in its thrall and made me its captive.

Jesus—my life, my peace—teach me to set my mind on You with even a hint of the determined and relentless focus with which Your mind is set on me.

18

*"I will make a covenant of peace with them;
it will be an everlasting covenant with them.
I will establish and multiply them, and will set
My sanctuary among them forever. My dwelling
place will be with them; I will be their God, and
they will be My people."*
—Ezekiel 37:26–27

*The Word became flesh and took up residence
among us.*
—John 1:14

MORNING

God with us, Immanuel, Your stated purpose for Your
Incarnation and all that it entailed—Your birth, Your
crucifixion, Your resurrection, Your ascension, the
sending of Your Spirit—was to establish peace.

You are Peace. The peace You offer is not something
separate from Yourself. The peace You offer is entirely
based on who You are. Who You are is all that matters.

When Your messenger came to Mary, as recorded
in Luke 1, Your message was a bit unsettling: "Do not
fear. I am about to upend your life and make you center
stage for My divine drama, but do not fear." Mary had
one question: *"How can this be?"* (v. 34). You had one
answer: *"The Holy Spirit will come upon you, and the
power of the Most High will overshadow you"* (v. 35).
Mary wanted to know *how*, but You only told her *who*.

"Our faith does not provide us with an answer, but with a Person. When Mary sought an explanation, what she got was a revelation," my son Brantley reminds me.

I can imagine how Mary might have reacted had You explained to her the *how* of Your plan. How would I respond to the most complex explanation of the most intricate matter regarding a subject of which I am wholly ignorant? That would sound like baby talk compared to an explanation about how You would come as a little baby fashioned in the womb of a virgin. The *how* would not have brought peace to Mary's heart, but the *who* caused a peace that surpassed understanding to stand guard over her heart (Philippians 4:7).

When anxiety tries to lay claim to my thoughts, when fear seeks a foothold in my mind, when confusion threatens to make a stand in my heart, I look to You, I seek Your face. You are all the antidote I need to anything that might steal my peace.

You will keep in perfect peace
the mind that is dependent on You,
for it is trusting in You.
Trust in the LORD forever,
because in Yah, the LORD, is an everlasting rock!
—Isaiah 26:3–4

-------- **THOUGHT FOR THE DAY** --------
You are all the antidote I need
to anything that might steal my peace.

EVENING

You came to me. You, the Unknowable made Yourself known. The Invisible made Yourself visible. The Invulnerable made Yourself vulnerable. The Unapproachable approached.

No frantic seeking was required. No ceremonies and rituals were necessary. You, for whom our souls long, long for us. You have made Yourself findable. *"'You will seek me and find me when you seek me with all your heart. I will be found by you,' declares the Lord"* (Jeremiah 29:13–14 NIV). With all our anxious looking about, You were always there. Your presence is peace.

I found You in the spaces in between
I found You in the dark and not the light
I looked for You in drama
In the earthquake and the fire
And found You in the quiet,
You were waiting for me there.
I looked for You in miracles
In the loud, in voices raised
I looked for You in gatherings
In signs, in prayer and praise
But I found You in the gentle breeze
The still small voice, the darkened cave.

I found You in the spaces
Between sleeping and awake
I found You in the waiting
The worry, in the fear

I found You in the sleepless night
I found You in despair
I found You in the questions
No loud answers anywhere
I found You in the silence
Silence full not silence void
I found You in the spaces
You were looking for me there.
—Rachel Holley

Because of our God's merciful compassion, the Dawn from on high will visit us...to guide our feet into the way of peace.
—Luke 1:78–79

If possible, on your part, live at peace with everyone.
—Romans 12:18

Let the peace of Christ rule in your hearts, since as members of one body you were called to peace.
—Colossians 3:15 (NIV)

MORNING

Peace is a pursuit. You say of the righteous person, ***"He must seek peace and pursue it"*** (1 Peter 3:11). Peace is active, not passive.

Word made flesh, You have come to put our feet on the way of peace, to lead us in ways of living that bring peace. When I consider how You were willing to humble Yourself fully so that You could bring to us the gift of Your peace, I am confronted with the many ways that I will not humble myself even slightly to bring peace.

During this Christmas season, I have found myself captured by the words of the classic hymn "Let There Be Peace on Earth" by Jill Jackson and Sy Miller. "Let there be peace on earth, and let it begin with me." These words may be derived from the Prayer of St. Francis of Assisi, "Lord, make me an instrument of Your peace." So, I think, living in this world, in the midst of strife and anger, what would it mean for me to be an instrument of Your peace?

Our world is more than ever defined by our conflicts: accusations, punches and counterpunches, rhetoric growing increasingly shrill until reason and truth are left trampled, and collateral damage in the war of slogans and talking points.

Bring the focus in tighter. Little arguments, petty responses later regretted, disagreements blown out of proportion, and hurt feelings, nurtured and fed, occur in abundance.

Let peace begin with me.

It takes on a new look as I view it through the prism of my everyday circumstances. When I let it become something more than a Christmas sentiment, it loses its soft focus, and I find it to be all sharp edges and harsh angles, demanding outrageous grace and humility that is beyond me. What about when Christmas is safely packed away and out of sight for another year, will I keep the reality of Christmas unpacked in my life? Will I be an instrument of Your peace?

Now, whether I am shining the light of these words on the world or on my country or on my family or on people whose lives intersect with mine at any juncture, the picture changes—the light falls on me. The focus is no longer on others and what they might have done to deserve my anger. The focus is now on me and what I can do to be an instrument of Your peace.

Outrageous grace. Humility that is beyond me. I have no other way for peace to begin with me, than for peace to begin in me. Dying to pride, yielding control, I must allow peace to flow from me like rivers of living water.

What is Your call on my life? Peace: *"Since as members of one body you were **called to peace**"* (Colossians 3:15 NIV; emphasis added). Can I mouth words about "God's call" and not offer myself to be an instrument of Your peace?

Make me an instrument of Your peace.

--------- **THOUGHT FOR THE DAY** ---------
Make me an instrument of Your peace.

EVENING
Peace that is *in* me becomes the peace that comes *through* me.

Prince of Peace, how can I let Your peace rule me? How can I allow the peace You bring to be the defining element of my personality?

The result of righteousness will be peace; the effect of righteousness will be quiet confidence forever.
—Isaiah 32:17

Righteousness and peace kiss each other.
—Psalm 85:10 (NIV)

Lord Jesus, Prince of Peace, as I pursue the peace You offer, it leads me to the righteousness You require. You came to earth in Your baby form, grew to manhood, and offered Your life *for* me on the Cross so that You could offer Your life *to* me through Your Spirit. You have given me Your righteousness, imparted as a gift. Let me put that righteousness more and more on display. Let me find the complete surrender to You that results in righteousness. Then, I will have found peace. Then I will have found the life I was made for. The peace that righteousness creates in me can be the gift of peace I give to those around me. The work of righteousness in me compels me to instigate peace, offer peace, and impose peace, no matter the battering my pride might take.

Focusing on You in the season of Your birth, I cannot escape the knowledge that I often choose my pride over Your peace and some-times believe my thoughts over Your Word, giving doubt and fear an opening. I pray that You will keep me aware that the way of peace leads through the demands of righteousness.

> The house of my soul is too small for you to enter: make it more spacious by your coming. It lies in ruins: rebuild it. Some things are to be found there that offend your gaze; I confess this to be so and know it well. But who will clean my house? To whom but yourself can I cry, Cleanse me of hidden sins, O Lord, and for those incurred through others, pardon your servant?
> —Augustine, *The Confessions*, book 1.5.6

When Christ came, He proclaimed the good news of peace to you who were far away and peace to those who were near.
—Ephesians 2:17

Suddenly there was a multitude of the heavenly host with the angel, praising God and saying: Glory to God in the highest heaven, and peace on earth to people He favors!
—Luke 2:13–14

MORNING

What a concert You arranged for a few unnamed shepherds!

I think of the most beautiful voices on earth singing the grandest piece of music ever composed. The sound of the perfectly pitched and supremely resonant voices creates awe and elicits from the audience strong emotions, tears, and applause. Even when the concert is over, the music finished, the listeners' emotions remain stirred. So I cannot even imagine how heaven's voices proclaiming the eternal song must have sounded.

No one on earth has ever heard such a thing, except those shepherds *"keeping watch over their flock by night"* (Luke 2:8 NKJV).

What are the lyrics in the angels' song of salvation? A proclamation of peace! Peace that had never been available on earth was, in the presence of the shepherds, offered freely from heaven. This peace was something brand-new, never heard of before, never experienced in history—peace that only heaven knew, now offered to people on earth.

Heaven came to earth in the form of a baby. With Your birth, heaven's rich storehouse of peace was opened and offered to earth's inhabitants. It took a chorus of angels, with voices sweeter than any ever heard before on earth, to make such an announcement: in the highest heaven, glory to God; on earth, peace to its people.

I imagine the scene when those honored shepherds found You, lying in a manger inside a stable. It was a place familiar to them—the place where little lambs were born, a place with smells and sounds they knew, a place where they felt at home, perhaps. And there, they encountered the Lamb of God.

They must have been ecstatic as they told the story to Mary and Joseph. They were not men of lofty words. How could they express the wonder that the angels had told them about a newborn baby, and it sounded like singing to their ears? How could they convey their amazement that the King had been born in a place where they felt at home and welcomed?

Who would believe them if they told the story of how they, lowly shepherds, had been the first to hear the rhythms of redemption?

If You chose the lowliest of men to hear the announcement of heaven's proudest moment, then make me lowly. I choose not to seek the praise of people, but rather to crave the lowliest place, from which I can hear You clearly. To bow at Your feet is my highest aspiration. Here is where I can hear the song of the ages: glory to God and peace to people on earth.

-------- **THOUGHT FOR THE DAY** --------
To bow at Your feet is my highest aspiration.

EVENING

If I am not careful, my world gets very small: my, mine, I, me, here, and now. Your unfathomable act of love, which we celebrate as Christmas, had no such boundaries. Eternity's proclamation of peace was to those far away as well as to those nearby.

Those far away. Sometimes even those who are geographically near me are far away to me. Certainly those whose language is strange to me and whose faces are unknown to me sometimes exist only on the outermost edges of my awareness.

But with my mind's eye, I look into Your precious face and remember that You so wanted to bring peace to those near and those far away—to the people of the world—that You left the highest place in heaven to come to the lowest place on earth. How can I dismiss Your great desire so I can satisfy my selfishness?

Remind me that celebrating Christmas is so much more than traditions and presents and decorations and lights. Surely it is no celebration for You when those things take priority, and the celebration of You is reduced to mindless platitudes and pretty pictures on Christmas cards. The Christmas season, the holiday to which we have reduced it, tends to reverse the focus You mean for us to have. The very nature of our holiday turns us to me, mine, I, me, here, and now.

Prince of Peace, here is my heart. Fill my heart with what fills Your heart. Fill it with the world of people You love. I want to celebrate You in ways that bring You pleasure. Let no one be far away to me.

*We have been rescued from our enemies'
clutches, to serve Him without fear in holiness
and righteousness in His presence all our days.*
—Luke 1:74–75

*How long will I store up anxious concerns
within me, agony in my mind every day? How
long will my enemy dominate me?*
—Psalm 13:2

MORNING

Zechariah prophesied that first Advent, under the
influence of Your Spirit. He prophesied about the
peace Your salvation promised: *"We have been rescued
from our enemies' clutches, to serve Him without fear
in holiness and righteousness in His presence all our
days."*

Your Incarnation brought into being a salvation so
full and complete that it reaches to the deepest parts of
me. The peace Your salvation offers rescues me from
the anxious concerns and agony of mind that are my
enemies. Those enemies in the spiritual realm are just
as real as enemies with flesh and blood. They present a
different kind of danger, a different kind of assault, but
are destructive and death-dealing in their own way.

You came to earth because I have a spiritual enemy
who is bent on my destruction. It is that very enemy You
came to conquer. That enemy uses lies as his weapon
against me—lies that, when I embrace them, lead to
anxious concerns within me and agony in my mind. You

came to earth to go behind enemy lines and engage in hand-to-hand combat with my adversary on my behalf.

Your battle gear looked to those on earth like the soft skin of a newborn baby. But nothing could have been more devastating to the enemy seeking my defeat. You invaded his territory. You staged a surprise rescue operation. You assaulted his base camp and released his prisoners of war.

Prince of Peace, this peace You have offered me was won with the shedding of Your blood. You, who could have stayed above the fray, instead entered in full force.

Celebrating Christmas this year, I celebrate that my enemy cannot dominate me. Jesus, I celebrate that You have rescued me from my enemies' clutches, and I will serve You without fear, in holiness and righteousness, in Your presence all my days.

Glory to God in the highest heaven,
and peace on earth to people He favors!
—Luke 2:14

-------- **THOUGHT FOR THE DAY** --------
You came to earth to go behind enemy lines
and engage in hand-to-hand combat
with my adversary on my behalf.

Evening

When I allow my enemy room to maneuver, and give his lies a place to land, I am turning my back on the gift of Your Incarnation. The fierce battle, the heroic rescue, the great cost—all to redeem me from the clutches of my enemy—are then wasted in my behalf…. Forgive me, Jesus, when I so dishonor my salvation.

> *He reached down from on high*
> *and took hold of me;*
> *He pulled me out of deep waters.*
> *He rescued me from my powerful enemy*
> *and from those who hated me,*
> *for they were too strong for me.*
> —Psalm 18:16–17

In this season, let me remember that I am freed from any hold the enemy may ever have had on me because You have reached down from on high and taken hold of me. Your reach was not just putting out Your hand for me to grasp. You jumped into my deep waters with both feet. You came right down into my muck and yuck and grabbed hold of me.

> *He was pierced because of our transgressions,*
> *crushed because of our iniquities;*
> *punishment for our peace was on Him,*
> *and we are healed by His wounds.*
> —Isaiah 53:5

Warrior King, Prince of Peace, born in a stable, laid in a manger, I thank You…. Thank You, thank You, thank You.

Just for Love's Sake Our Redeemer Yielded His Throne for a Manger

In the same region, shepherds were staying out in the fields and keeping watch at night over their flock. Then an angel of the Lord stood before them, and the glory of the Lord shone around them, and they were terrified. But the angel said to them, "Don't be afraid, for look, I proclaim to you good news of great joy that will be for all the people: today a Savior, who is Messiah the Lord, was born for you in the city of David. This will be the sign for you: you will find a baby wrapped snugly in cloth and lying in a feeding trough."

—Luke 2:8–12

MORNING

Good news of great joy. A Savior was born *for you*! the angels declared.

Shepherds, unknown, unnoticed. For them, a Savior.

After their journey to the King, the shepherds returned to their flock. They kept watch over their flock the rest of the night. They did the same thing the next night, and the next, and the next. They did not become famous or rich. Their lot in life did not change—except that now they had the gift of joy. So, really, everything changed.

The joy You brought to earth had nothing at all to do with the outward circumstances of our lives. You did not promise that everything would go easily and well and that would make us joyful. You promised just the opposite: You said that the world will hate us (John 15:19) and that in the world, we will have sorrow

(John 16:20). But in You, we are also promised joy, *"great joy."*

This gift of joy so excited the heavenlies that the great veil that hides heaven from earth's sight was pulled back just a crack, and the glory of the Lord shone around the shepherds. So momentous was this event that heaven made the announcement rather than having it delivered through the mouths of prophets. News of great joy!

This joy is of such importance that its declaration had been planned from before the earth was formed. It had to be presented in accordance with its value. It was a gift so precious that the very heavens would open for its presentation.

But this joy has nothing to do with what is going on in my life. The joy You have given me is so valuable to me *because* it does not change with the circumstances. It is a joy that has taken up residence in me and stays in place through the roughest storms.

Lord Jesus, You are the joy of my heart. In Your presence is fullness of joy. I do not have to wait on the circumstances to line up just right. You are the gift of great joy.

--------- **THOUGHT FOR THE DAY** ---------
Your joy takes up residence in me
and stays in place through the roughest storms.

EVENING

The shepherds were not expecting a heavenly announcement of Messiah's birth that night as they kept watch over their flock. It had never occurred to them that they might be the recipients of the birth announcement of the King of kings. They were not watching the sky carefully, looking for a sign. They had not studied for years, anticipating Your coming. But You came to them anyway.

The wise men were just the opposite. They had been watching for the sign of Your birth and their studies had led them to anticipate it soon. They had been looking for You and expecting You. And You came to them, also.

You can read a heart.

Whether a person is articulate and learned, or simple and inar-ticulate, You can see the hearts that long for Your appearing. You are not put off by either. What comes from the lips matters little to You. What comes from the heart is everything.

Joy can be born in any life at any time. All it takes is a ready heart.

Jesus, thank You that Your requirements to receive Your gift are uncomplicated. Thank You that neither the sophistication of the wise men nor the simplicity of the shepherds made any difference at all to You.

Your *"good news of great joy"* is *"for all the people."*

"I have spoken these things to you so that
My joy may be in you and your joy may be
complete."
—John 15:11

Jesus, ready my heart to receive the full gift of
Your joy.

My soul proclaims the greatness of the Lord,
and my spirit has rejoiced in God my Savior,
because He has looked with favor
on the humble condition of His slave.
—Luke 1:46–48

MORNING

I wonder what Mary's thoughts were like the day before Gabriel arrived with Your amazing announcement. I wonder what she was pondering in the hour and the minutes before You interrupted her life. How suddenly everything can be altered.

Mary, a pious young girl who loved You and longed for Your salvation, lived quietly in Nazareth. You had called and appointed her for this great task even before the world was created. Through all the generations, You had little Mary in view. You created her at just the right time, gave her to just the right parents, established her in just the right tribe and housed her in just the right village. You betrothed her to just the right man at just the right season.

On that day, You seemed to come suddenly, without preamble, out of nowhere, without warning. But in reality You had been creating this moment and laying its framework from the time You first planned for redemption.

In the blink of an eye, Mary was taken out of her ordinary life and thrust into salvation's story. But the action had been in process since before time. During all those years and generations when it seemed You were withholding the Redeemer, You were really in the process of sending the Redeemer.

In a matter of seconds, Mary learned about Your call on her life, and she was immediately flooded with a joy before unknown to her. Her spirit rejoiced and her soul proclaimed God's greatness. Joy bubbled up from her innermost being. She had a role in salvation's story.

You have a call on my life—a purpose for which You created me and placed me and positioned me on the earth. You have looked with favor on the humble condition of this slave. The joy You brought to earth as a gift for Your people is ignited when Your purpose is revealed. To know that You have factored me into Your plan for redemption stirs in me such great joy that my very spirit rejoices.

---------- ## THOUGHT FOR THE DAY ----------

The joy You brought to earth as a gift for Your people
is ignited when Your purpose is revealed.
Reveal Your purpose to me today.

EVENING

"My soul proclaims the greatness of the Lord."

I want that to be my song. I want that to be my story. I want my soul—all that I am—I want my soul to proclaim Your greatness.

Why do I cling stubbornly to the ways of my flesh and my human nature when there is joy waiting for me just beyond them? Why do I mouth surrender, but then stubbornly go my own way, when true yieldedness is where my joy is found? *"Direct me in the path of your commands, for there I find delight"* (Psalm 119:35 NIV).

Jesus, let my life house You. Make Yourself at home in me. Recreate me so completely that only You are evident. When I am being my most authentic, unvarnished self, let it be You that shows. Let my soul proclaim Your greatness.

The evidence of Your indwelling presence is true joy. Not so much high emotion as calm and settled contentment. The joy You have birthed in me acclimates my spiritual vision so that I can see the *"treasures of darkness"* and the *"riches stored in secret places"* (Isaiah 45:3 NIV). When nothing in my life seems reason for rejoicing, I still find myself rejoicing. I can see that You are at work, even in the darkest times, showing me the treasures that are only found in darkness and the riches that must be mined at great cost.

I long for more of You and less of me. Jesus, let Your fullness be formed in me, even if the birthing pains are long and hard. Teach me the depth of surrender that brought You, the eternal Son, to be born in a stable. Work in me the full measure of Your obedience that brought You, Creator and Sustainer, to die on the Cross.

> *Keeping our eyes on Jesus, the source and perfecter of our faith, who for the joy that lay before Him endured a cross and despised the shame, and has sat down at the right hand of God's throne.*
> —Hebrews 12:2

My soul proclaims Your greatness.

Immediately his mouth was opened and his tongue set free, and he began to speak, praising God.
—Luke 1:64

MORNING

The moment of Zechariah's obedience—an obedience gestated in silence—released the praise through his mouth that had been building in his heart.

Stripped of voice, Zechariah had learned to have no audience but You. He must also have been deaf, since his friends and neighbors had to motion to him to communicate (Luke 1:62). He had no conversation except with You. He heard no voices other than Yours.

When the time was right and You had brought to completion that which was being formed in Zechariah, You loosed his tongue and all the words stored up were released in a torrent of praise and joy.

When distractions are gone and the only focus is You, there is no other response. In Your presence, with Christ in full view and salvation on display, praise rises naturally from a full heart. Your words are true and right and pure. When all the other voices are silenced and You speak, the clarity Your voice brings calls for but one response.

My lips pour out praise,
for You teach me Your statutes.
My tongue sings about Your promise,
for all Your commandments are righteous.
—Psalm 119:171–172

I seek silence so I can pursue You without distraction. This Christmas season, at those times when You call me into Your presence, I choose to walk away from noise so that I will hear no voice but Yours. Let Your words spoken in Your voice generate genuine joy that finds its expression in the praises of my mouth.

---------- **THOUGHT FOR THE DAY** ----------

I seek silence so I can pursue You without distraction.

EVENING

When joy overflows, its conduit is praise. You have designed us so that the expression of our joy is essential to our experience of joy. Who can hold in joy? Who can keep joy bottled up? It insists on expression. Joy is consummated in praise.

When Zechariah opened his mouth for the first time in nine months, his first words were praise. Praise is what his tongue set free spoke.

> *My lips will shout for joy*
> *when I sing praise to You,*
> *because You have redeemed me.*
> *Therefore, my tongue will proclaim*
> *Your righteousness all day long.*
> —Psalm 71:23–24

On this night, Christmas Eve, when the crescendo of excitement over tomorrow's celebration is reached, keep me focused. Keep me aware of why I am celebrating. In the recesses of my heart, let joy find its fullness as I home in on You.

As I enjoy the prospect of the excitement my gifts to those I love will bring tomorrow, and as I anticipate the look of delight on their faces as they tear the wrappings open to reveal the perfect gift, I wonder if it is a faint echo and pale shadow of Your sense of anticipation on that night long ago just before Your great Gift was revealed.

Did You reproduce some facet of Your own joy in Zechariah in those months of buildup to Your great gift giving? Did Zechariah's explosion of praise after months in silence before You give a hint at Your stupendous joy?

Lord, I am delighted beyond words with the Gift You have bestowed. Every day I unwrap more of the ineffable, unspeakable, inexpressible Gift—every discovery adding more and more and more to my salvation experience. Since my tongue cannot form the words to express my praise adequately, tune Your ear to the joy that fills my heart.

Thanks be to God for His indescribable gift.
—2 Corinthians 9:15

MORNING

Before the celebrations begin, let me turn my heart to You.

No gift has ever been so costly.

No gift has ever been so treasured.

No gift has ever been so precious.

No gift has ever been so perfectly suited to both my needs and desires.

Each gift that I give today only faintly reflects the part of Your nature that makes giving joyous.

Each gift that I receive today reminds me that I have received the most profound Gift that can ever be given, and I am filled with gratitude.

The joy I feel, as I am warmed by the presence of those I love, is nothing compared to the joy I have because You have fulfilled Your promise from of old and have given Your Son to be my Savior.

I rejoice over Your promise like one who finds vast treasure.
—Psalm 119:162

Today we will ooh and aah; we will hug and laugh and remember. We will enjoy each other's presence. But You will be at the center of every thought. You will be taking pleasure in our company, as we take pleasure in Yours.

I pray this blessing over those whom You have placed into my life today: *"Now may the God of hope fill you with all joy and peace in believing, so that you may overflow with hope by the power of the Holy Spirit"* (Romans 15:13).

·········· THOUGHT FOR THE DAY ··········
We will enjoy each other's presence.
But You will be at the center of every thought.

EVENING

As another Christmas day celebration comes to a close, I realize that the Christmas spirit will pass, being stored away until another December 25. But the Spirit of Christ indwells me forever.

As I have celebrated this season with Christ in view, the wonder of Your redemption has been revived in me. You are not a season or a holiday or a hymn or a decoration. I sometimes let the glory of my salvation be overshadowed by the gloss of Christmas. But this season, my heart is fixed on You, and I pray that You will refresh the joy of my salvation 365 days a year. *"Bring joy to your servant, for to you, O Lord, I lift up my soul"* (Psalm 86:4 NIV).

This Christmas night, I consider what Your birth has made possible, and I ponder You.

> Behold—what Man is this
> Whose Voice the winds obey
> Whose touch can make the leper clean
> And wash his shame away
>
> Behold—what Love is this
> That reaches out for me
> And lifts me from the miry clay
> To set my spirit free
>
> Behold—what Pow'r is this
> That shatters sin's domain
> And clears away all hindrance to
> The mighty Savior's reign

Behold—the Lamb of God
Who takes my sin away
Behold His nail-pierced hands and feet—
The print of God on clay

Behold—our reigning Lord
All glory, honor, might
Belong to Him—the worthy One
Now clothed in robes of light

Behold—our coming King
All peoples, every tongue
Sing out His praise, lift high His Name
The final vict'ry's won

Since the children have flesh and blood in common, He also shared in these, so that through His death He might destroy the one holding the power of death—that is, the Devil—and free those who were held in slavery all their lives by the fear of death. For it is clear that He does not reach out to help angels, but to help Abraham's offspring. Therefore He had to be like His brothers in every way, so that He could become a merciful and faithful high priest in service to God, to make propitiation for the sins of the people.
—Hebrews 2:14–17

MORNING

Your Gift comes in such creative wrapping.

Yesterday morning, Christmas day, beautifully wrapped gifts were piled high around the Christmas tree. With some of the gifts, as much thought had been given to the wrapping of the gift as to the selection of gift itself. Sometimes the wrapping was meant to disguise the gift so the surprise would be all the greater. A small gift being wrapped and hidden inside a big box.

Yesterday, the artistry of the wrappings made the anticipation of the gifts greater. The wrappings invited us into the gifts.

Today, the wrappings are gone and the gifts are the main focus.

You wrapped Your gift in flesh and blood. The wrapping was such that it invited us into the Gift. Had You sent Your Son unwrapped, we could not have seen

Him because the brightness of His countenance would have blinded us. Like the Israelites of old, we would have hidden our faces from Him in fear and shame.

The angels know Him wrapped in eternal glory and royal robes. They saw Him before He took upon Himself the form of a servant and was made in the likeness of men. The angels saw His triumphant return to the glory He had before the world began, and see Him now in His exalted form.

But we see Him in the flawless beauty of His humanity. We see the grandeur of His Incarnation, when He demonstrated the enormity of His love for us by wrapping Himself in flesh and blood so that He could destroy that which held us captive. Seeing Him, we are blinded by His beauty to anything other than Him.

We will someday see Your indescribable Gift as the angels see Him. I know that sight will be a different beauty than I have ever known. But I cannot imagine that it will be more breathtakingly beautiful to me than the King of kings wrapped in flesh and blood for my sake.

--------- ## THOUGHT FOR THE DAY ---------
Seeing You, I am blinded by Your beauty
to anything other than You.

Evening

You reach out to help those whom You have created. You, who created, can as easily recreate.

You, who needed nothing, entered earth as a tiny baby, needing everything. You, who never had to feel hunger or cold or pain or exhaustion, chose to share in my lot for redemption's sake. Glory was hidden behind flesh. Power was dressed in infant helplessness; majesty, wrapped in swaddling clothes.

You came to participate in our humanity so that we, first made in the image of God, could be remade in the image of Christ. You chose to be made like us in every way so You could secure our salvation.

As the Christmas celebration begins to fade into the background until next year, I embrace the reality of the Incarnation we honor. "The mystery of Christ's incarnation is to be adored, not pried into," stated Matthew Henry in his commentary on the Book of Matthew. I am the living proof of Your salvation. Your power to recreate, to turn brokenness into beauty, is on display in my life. Every day, I experience Your redemption, and I adore You; and I adore Your Incarnation, because Your entrance into my life allows me to be in a constant state of renewing.

Broken into Beautiful *(chorus)*
You change worthless into precious
Guilty to forgiven
Hungry into satisfied
Empty into full
All the lies are shattered
And we believe we matter
When You change broken into beautiful

—BROKEN INTO BEAUTIFUL, Sue Smith / Chad Cates
/ Gwen Smith
© 2006 New Spring, Inc / CCTB Music / Upper Cates
Music / Sunday Best Music

He will be named Wonderful Counselor.
—Isaiah 9:6

MORNING

Nothing occurs in my life for which You do not have all wisdom, knowledge, and understanding. The Incarnation, through which You made Yourself accessible to me, means that You can impart to me any wisdom I need.

> *Now if any of you lacks wisdom, he should ask God, who gives to all generously and without criticizing, and it will be given to him.*
> —James 1:5

I lay before You now all the decisions awaiting resolution, all the yet unseen events that will require that I choose a behavior or find the right words today, the determination about how I will spend the minutes of this day—everything this day holds. I ask now for Your wisdom, Wonderful Counselor.

I choose now to surrender to Your wisdom, spoken to my understanding by Your Spirit incarnate in me. Your wisdom will most often lead me to do, be, and say the exact opposite of what my flesh is inclined to do, be, and say. In advance, I choose You.

Today I want to live fully in that which Your Incarnation has made possible. Remind me about the gift of Your presence, Wonderful Counselor. Let my joyful heart be attuned to Your voice.

I am teaching you the way of wisdom;
I am guiding you on straight paths.
When you walk, your steps will not be hindered;
when you run, you will not stumble.
Hold on to instruction; don't let go.
Guard it, for it is your life.
—Proverbs 4:11–13

———— THOUGHT FOR THE DAY ————
Today I want to live fully
in that which Your Incarnation has made possible.

EVENING

In Your Incarnation, You brought everything You are and everything heaven has into the grasp of earth's inhabitants. Because of Your salvation, I do not have to limit my responses to what I can perceive or what I can anticipate or what I can formulate. You have made Yourself available to me every second of every day. Unending, unbroken fellowship with You is available to me. You have made Your home in me. Everything You have, You will make available on my behalf.

> *Wisdom and strength belong to God;*
> *counsel and understanding are His.*
> —Job 12:13

Wonderful Counselor, let Your wisdom and understanding be worked out in my circumstances. Wean me from my dependence upon my own ideas and understanding and perceptions. Free me from the notion that I might possess any wisdom that is my own.

I want the wisdom and understanding that are a direct deposit from Your heart to mine. I want to have Your words in my mouth and Your understanding in my mind. Teach me to wait on You before I spurt words into a situation. Teach me to wait on You before I make up my mind about a matter. May the following words be true of me: *"My mouth speaks wisdom; my heart's meditation brings understanding"* (Psalm 49:3).

Wonderful Counselor, I rejoice in Your wisdom.

I am overjoyed to realize that I can draw upon Your eternal reservoir of wisdom and understanding.

I celebrate Christmas daily because Your presence in me surprises me every day by what You bring to every challenge, every circumstance, every interaction. Because of You, I am ever unwrapping new and precious gifts.

He will be named . . . Mighty God.
—Isaiah 9:6

MORNING

Jesus, let me know You as Mighty God. Speak into my heart and mind and soul that You are Mighty God and all power is in Your hand. Your words live in me and redefine me. I am never a victim of circumstances. I am never a captive of events. Because You are Mighty God.

> *God is our refuge and strength,*
> *a helper who is always found*
> *in times of trouble.*
> *Therefore we will not be afraid,*
> *though the earth trembles*
> *and the mountains topple*
> *into the depths of the seas,*
> *though its waters roar and foam*
> *and the mountains quake with its turmoil.*
> —Psalm 46:1–3

You are the Fear Chaser. Sovereign Ruler over both heaven and earth, You sought me out to offer me Yourself. You bring all Your power and might to my rescue.

When events threaten to overwhelm me, when circumstances beyond my control seem to pound my life like ocean waves, when I feel assaulted by life's twists and turns, I cry out to You, Mighty God.

I have joy knowing that no matter what happens *around* me, nothing can happen *to* me, nothing can happen *in* me over which You are not Mighty God.

--------- **Thought for the Day** ---------
I have joy knowing that
no matter what happens *around* me,
nothing can happen *to* me,
nothing can happen *in* me
over which You are not Mighty God.

EVENING

Mighty God, You are the one God who is above all power and dominion, above all rule and authority. You are the all-powerful God who created the earth with nothing but Your Word, who manages its rotations and its paths with Your own power. Mighty, Mighty God.

You—all might, tempered with love and compelled by compassion—came to earth in the fullness of time to save Your people from their sins.

Jesus, when my mind's eye sees You wrapped in swaddling clothes and lying in a manger, I am overwhelmed with the wonder that You would bring Your eternal might, Your unrivaled power, Your unparalleled and unchallenged strength to earth to use it on my behalf.

The fact that Your love would drive You to take on earth's forms and fashion Yourself as a man awakens wonder in my heart this evening.

As I move through the final days of the celebration of Christmas, I see the tree's limbs are now limp and the wrappings, ribbons, and bows have been rumpled, torn, and discarded. Already my mind leaps ahead to the days when the hoopla has all come to an end, when the guests have all gone home and the ornaments are stored away and the lights boxed up, when life settles back into its regular rhythms.

Help my heart stay steady. Show me daily the meaning of the Incarnation—that You, Mighty God, have taken up my cause; that You, Mighty God, are my defender, my protector, my advocate; that You, Mighty God, are living in me, incarnate in my lowly flesh, demonstrating Your all-powerfulness for me. You have made Yourself so available to me that nothing can put any space between us.

Who can separate us from the love of Christ?
Can affliction or anguish or persecution
*   or famine or nakedness or danger or sword?*
As it is written:
*   Because of You we are being put to death*
*   all day long; we are counted as sheep to be*
*   slaughtered.*
No, in all these things we are more than victorious
*   through Him who loved us.*
For I am persuaded that neither death nor life,
*   nor angels nor rulers,*
*   nor things present, nor things to come, nor powers,*
*   nor height, nor depth, nor any other created thing*
*   will have the power to separate us*
*   from the love of God that is in Christ Jesus*
*   our Lord!*
—Romans 8:35–39

He will be named... Eternal Father.
—Isaiah 9:6

Morning

When Your Son revealed Your nature more clearly to us by taking up residence among us, Your tenderness came into view. Through the lens of the Law, You appeared to be demanding and exacting. What a wonderful surprise when the Gift You gave fully revealed Your tenderness, Your mercy, and Your gentle love for Your people.

Jesus, whose name is Eternal Father, keeping Your children safe. Making sure Your children are provided for. Calling Your children into Your presence just for the joy of it.

We would not have guessed that You, the God who rules heaven and earth, long for us to know You as Father.

Eternal Father. That name casts light on so much that had been hidden. Father—Protector, Defender, Guide, Provider, Teacher.

> *"The Lord your God who goes before you will fight for you, just as you saw Him do for you in Egypt. And you saw in the wilderness how the Lord your God carried you as a man carries his son all along the way you traveled until you reached this place."*
> —Deuteronomy 1:30–31

Eternal Father, I yield myself to Your tender care. Correct me when I treat You as someone whose presence is fearful or whose temperament is cross and critical instead of as my Eternal Father.

As You teach me Your name and help me learn about Your true nature, I crave Your presence and find there my greatest joy and peace. I see You carrying me as a father carries his child.

Who but an Eternal Father would move heaven and earth to save me? Who but an Eternal Father would pay any price and make any sacrifice for my redemption? Who but an Eternal Father would be aware of my needs before I am? Who but an Eternal Father would hear my cry before it escapes my lips? Who but an Eternal Father would be so attentive to my every sigh?

Let me experience You as Eternal Father in my life today.

---------- **THOUGHT FOR THE DAY** ----------
Eternal Father,
I yield myself to Your tender care.

EVENING

Eternal Father, You shape and mold the character of Your children.

"LORD, You are our Father; we are the clay, and You are our potter; we all are the work of Your hands."
—Isaiah 64:8

The potter sees in the lump of clay the vessel he is creating. With patient, hands-on work and careful attention to detail, he continuously envisions the finished work in his mind's eye. A father, as he shapes his child's character, can see ahead to what is coming into view.

Eternal Father, You see in me what I cannot see in myself. I often fail to recognize the pressure of Your hands molding me and shaping me. I think I am being pressed by circumstances or squeezed by need, but nothing touches my life except that which You can use to mold me into a vessel that contains You. Shaped not from the outside, but from the inside.

When You have molded some part of me so that it has the shape of You, then I am passed through the fire. Your fire sets the shape so that it is stable. Your fire does not consume; Your fire purifies and strengthens.

Eternal Father, shape me, mold me, sculpt me until I am the exact image of You.

The Spirit of the Lord GOD is on Me, because the LORD has anointed Me to bring good news to the poor. He has sent Me to heal the brokenhearted, to proclaim liberty to the captives, and freedom to the prisoners; to proclaim the year of the LORD's favor, and the day of our God's vengeance; to comfort all who mourn, to provide for those who mourn in Zion; to give them a crown of beauty instead of ashes, festive oil instead of mourning, and splendid clothes instead of despair. And they will be called righteous trees, planted by the LORD, to glorify Him.
—Isaiah 61:1–3

MORNING

God Most High, You have come in the form of flesh to lift up the lowly. Is there a more astonishing aspect to Your Incarnation than this?

I echo Mary's words: *"He has looked with favor on the humble condition of His slave"* (Luke 1:48). Those who are invisible in earth's societies are the very focus of Your redemption.

I claim my place with the poor, the brokenhearted, the captives, the prisoners, and those who mourn. Nothing that I own or possess in the earth can lift me out of the poverty of my spirit or the prison of my sin. Only You can.

This morning, I am trying to fathom that when You left heaven for earth, You did it for such a one as I. It was not as a reward to those who were saintly and deserving, but as a Redeemer for those who were fallen and completely undeserving.

You came intentionally taking the servant's role, not demanding to be treated as the King You are. *"The Son of Man did not come to be served, but to serve, and to give His life—a ransom for many"* (Matthew 20:28).

The kingly anointing on You, Messiah, was to do the work of heaven on earth. Little did we guess that heaven's highest work was aimed at earth's lowliest inhabitants.

I am undeserving, lowly, unworthy. I will shout it from the rooftops! It makes me the very target of Your loving salvation. O what joy!

--------- **THOUGHT FOR THE DAY** ---------
I claim my place with the poor,
the brokenhearted, the captives,
the prisoners, and those who mourn.

EVENING

Redeemer King, I long to be a righteous tree for the display of Your glory.

When You speak my name in the heavenlies, I want You to say something like this: *"He is like a tree planted beside streams of water that bears its fruit in season and whose leaf does not wither. Whatever he does prospers"* (Psalm 1:3).

I want You to describe me with these words:

> *"Blessed is the man who trusts in the LORD, whose confidence indeed is the LORD. He will be like a tree planted by water: it sends its roots out toward a stream, it doesn't fear when heat comes, and its foliage remains green. It will not worry in a year of drought or cease producing fruit."*
> —Jeremiah 17:7–8

A righteous tree, planted by the Lord—may that be a description of me. May all that You have done for me be evident to those who observe me. Show Yourself to anyone who looks my way. Take the spotlight. Occupy center stage.

Will heat show You best? Let there be heat.

Will drought show You best? Let there be drought.

You have planted me beside streams of water, and no matter what the conditions around me, my roots are in You, the Living Water. My leaf does not wither and my foliage remains green—because of You.

This is why You came to earth. You have looked with favor upon the humble condition of Your slave. You have turned my mourning into dancing and given me the garment of salvation. You have planted me as a tree in Your garden, and made me hearty and indestructible.

I exalt You, my Redeemer.

"I am the Alpha and the Omega," says the Lord God, "the One who is, who was, and who is coming, the Almighty."
—Revelation 1:8

Blessing and honor and glory and dominion
to the One seated on the throne,
and to the Lamb, forever and ever!
—Revelation 5:13

MORNING

With my mind's eye, I observe this glimpse into the glory that is Your natural habitat. I am all the more captivated by the thought of just how much You left behind when You took the form of a newborn baby to live out the Eternal Word in the realm of earth.

You left the heavens, where You were deemed worthy of all praise and honor and glory and dominion, to come to earth, where You were deemed worthy of death on the Cross. You left the heavens, where You heard the cries, *"Holy, holy, holy,"* to come to earth and hear people cry out, *"Crucify Him!"* (Revelation 4:8; Matthew 27:22–23). You left the heavens, where You were hailed as King, to come to earth, where You were derided and spat upon.

You are the One who is, who was, and who is coming. Your nature does not change between heaven and earth. The One who has always been is the very One who came to earth for my sake.

Heart of mine, look! Look at the majesty of the One who embraced humanity and took frail flesh as His robe. Compare the stable with the throne room. Compare the Cross with the throne. Magnificent love. Indescribable gift.

I join the hosts around Your throne this morning and joyfully sing, "Holy! Holy! Holy!"

-------- **THOUGHT FOR THE DAY** --------
I join the hosts around Your throne this morning
and joyfully sing, "Holy! Holy! Holy!"

EVENING

I have spent these days of Advent contemplating Your Incarnation. Like Mary, I treasure all these things in my heart (Luke 2:19).

My heart is full of joy. I will never lose the wonder of Your coming, as I remember the King in baby form, the Ruler in servant form, the Alpha and Omega, the One who has no beginning, who took on a beginning on the earth.

God with us.
The Word made flesh.
Wonderful Counselor.
Mighty God.
Eternal Father.
Prince of Peace.

With all I am, I worship You.

New Hope® Publishers is a division of WMU®, an international organization that challenges Christian believers to understand and be radically involved in God's mission. For more information about WMU, go to www.wmu.com. More information about New Hope books may be found at www.newhopedigital.com. New Hope books may be purchased at your local bookstore.

Use the QR reader on your
smartphone to visit us online at
www.newhopedigital.com

If you've been blessed by this book,
we would like to hear your story.
The publisher and author welcome your comments
and suggestions at: newhopereader@wmu.org.

ABOUT THE AUTHOR

Jennifer Kennedy Dean is the executive director of the Praying Life Foundation and a popular speaker and author. Best known as a gifted biblical expositor, Jennifer speaks regularly at national and international conferences and events and has taught for years at the Billy Graham Training Center at the Cove.

She has written and produced numerous books and multimedia Bible studies, including *Live a Praying Life, Fueled by Faith, Life Unhindered!, Legacy of Prayer, Secrets Jesus Shared, Heart's Cry, The Life-Changing Power in the Name of Jesus,* and *The Life-Changing Power in the Blood of Christ.* Notable authors, such as Beth Moore, Cynthia Heald, Nancy Leigh DeMoss, Bobbye Byerly, and Vicki Caruana, among others, have quoted her books. She has contributed numerous articles for *www.newhopedigital.com*, as well as Christian publications, such as *Decision, SpiritLed Woman,* and *Pray!*

Jennifer and her late husband, Wayne Dean, are the parents of three grown sons. She currently lives in Marion, Kentucky.

Books by Jennifer Kennedy Dean

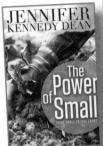

The Power of Small
Think Small to Live Large
978-1-59669-313-5

Secrets Jesus Shared
*Kingdom Insights Revealed
Through the Parables*
978-1-59669-108-7

Set Apart
*A 6-Week Study
of the Beatitudes*
978-1-59669-263-3

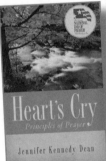

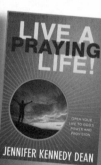

Heart's Cry
Principles of Prayer
978-1-59669-095-0

Life Unhindered!
Five Keys to Walking in Freedom
978-1-59669-286-2

Live a Praying Life!
*Open Your Life to God's
Plan and Provision*
978-1-59669-299-2

Available in bookstores everywhere.

For information about these books or any New Hope product,
visit www.newhopepublishers.com.